A Gift For:

_____

From:

_____

WIT AND WISDOM OF THE COWBOY

Jake Grogan

Kennebunkport, ME

TO MY FAMILY AND FRIENDS,
THANK YOU FOR MAKING EACH
DAY BETTER THAN THE LAST.

INTRODUCTION

From history to Hollywood, few figures have had the
lasting impact and significance in our society as
the American cowboy. We can all picture the character:
a Stetson-wearing, saloon-occupying gunslinger with
a quick tongue and an even quicker trigger finger.
He and his Wild Western culture are fascinating and
fun, so much so that we've all at one point wanted
to grow up to be a cowboy or cowgirl. So throw off
your inner city slicker and indulge yourself! Learn
how to speak, cook, think, and act like your favorite
Wild West legend. Grab your saddle and your spurs
because your adventure into the Wild West awaits!

"COURAGE IS BEING SCARED TO DEATH AND SADDLING UP ANYWAY."

— JOHN WAYNE

The monthly earnings for the average cowboy in the Wild West were between 25 and 40 dollars.

SCALAWAG

A mean or
worthless person

LONGRIDER

Somebody who had
to stay on the saddle
for an unusually
long time, usually
because the person
is on the run from
the authorities

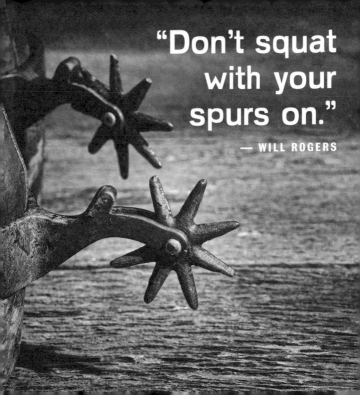

"Don't squat
with your
spurs on."

— WILL ROGERS

★ ★ ★

THE HARMONICA WAS THE INSTRUMENT OF CHOICE FOR MOST COWBOYS, MAINLY BECAUSE OF ITS SIZE AND PORTABILITY.

★ ★ ★

CONNIE DOUGLAS REEVES

(1901-2003)

Forced to withdraw from the University of Texas Law School because of the unstable economic climate brought on by the Great Depression, Reeves began working part time as a riding instructor at a stable in San Antonio. She would eventually move on to Camp Waldemar in Hunt, where she taught an estimated 30,000 girls how to ride horses. She married in 1942 and, for more than thirty years, managed a 10,000-acre sheep and cattle ranch with her husband while teaching young girls how to ride. She was inducted into the cowgirl Hall of Fame in 1997. Her passing came as a result of injuries sustained after being thrown from her horse.

WOLFER

A heavy drinker
or somebody with
a large appetite

YANNIGAN BAG

A bag in which cowboys kept
their personal belongings
while traveling

"A man's got to have a code, a creed to live by."

— JOHN WAYNE

A vehicle called the "Calf Wagon" was taken on some cattle drives to transport the newborn calves. The driver of this wagon was referred to as "Little Mary Cowboy."

"WESTERNS WERE ALWAYS MY FAVORITE THINGS WHEN I WAS LITTLE. AND IT ALWAYS BOTHERED ME WHEN COWBOYS WERE TOO CLEAN IN MOVIES, OR WHEN THEY WORE THEIR GUNS LIKE THEY HAD AN OUTFIT ON. IT ALWAYS WORKED BETTER WHEN A GUY LOOKED SWEATY AND SMELLY; I HADDA BELIEVE, I HADDA BELIEVE THAT."

— MICHAEL KEATON

CAHOOTS

A collaboration, often
of a secret or
questionable nature

"PUTTIN' ON A
COWBOY HAT &
A PAIR OF BOOTS
DOESN'T MAKE
YOU COUNTRY; LIKE
PUTTIN' ON A BALL
GOWN & GLASS HEELS
WON'T MAKE ME
CINDERELLA."

— KELLIE ELMORE

COWBOY BISCUITS

Makes 18

1 tsp. baking powder
1 c. all-purpose flour
¼ tsp. salt
2½ tbsp. shortening

½ c. water
1 tbsp. melted bacon
drippings

1 Preheat oven to 425 degrees. Using a large bowl, combine the baking powder, flour, and salt. While stirring, slowly pour the shortening in until the mixture resembles a coarse meal.

2 Sprinkle the water over the mixture while stirring until everything is moistened.

3 Shape the dough into 2" balls and place them on a lightly greased baking sheet. Brush the top of the dough balls with melted bacon drippings, adding as much or as little as you want to each biscuit.

4 Bake until the biscuits are browned, about 18 to 20 minutes.

THOUGH CATTLE COULD BE DRIVEN
TO COVER UP TO 25 MILES IN A
SINGLE DAY, THEIR WEIGHT WOULD
BE SO DRASTICALLY AFFECTED
THAT THEIR VALUE WOULD PLUMMET.
CATTLE DRIVERS, HAVING TO
SET ASIDE TIME EVERYDAY
TO ALLOW THE CATTLE TO GRAZE
AND FEED, OFTEN MAXED OUT
THEIR DAILY DISTANCE AT 15 MILES.
THIS OFTEN ADDED ENTIRE WEEKS
TO A GIVEN CATTLE DRIVE.

BILLY THE KID

(1859–1881)

One of the earliest outlaws to achieve a national profile, William H. Bonney first gained notoriety as a member of the famed Regulators, a deputized posse that fought in the Lincoln County War. His crime spree, ended by Sheriff Pat Garrett, saw the deaths of several deputies, one sheriff, a blacksmith, and two escapees from prison.

GROWLERS

Cans, pitchers, or buckets carried,
often by children, to the saloon
to be filled with beer and returned
to the workplace. The name
originates from the sound that it
makes when slid across the bar.

"EVERYBODY WAS
WEARING RHINESTONES,
ALL THOSE SPARKLY
CLOTHES, AND COWBOY
BOOTS. I DECIDED
TO WEAR A BLACK
SHIRT AND PANTS AND
SEE IF I COULD GET
BY WITH IT. I DID AND
I'VE WORN BLACK
CLOTHES EVER SINCE."

— JOHNNY CASH

"Mounted on my favorite horse, my lariat near my hand, and my trusty gun in my belt, I felt I could defy the world."

— NAT LOVE

BOWLERS AND TOP HATS WERE
THE HEADGEAR OF CHOICE IN
THE WILD WEST; THAT IS, UNTIL
HOLLYWOOD POPULARIZED THE
OVERSIZED TEN-GALLON HATS.
SILENT FILM STARS LIKE
TIM MCCOY DONNED THEM ON
SCREEN, THE RESULT OF WHICH
WAS THEIR BECOMING AN
ESSENTIAL PART OF FRONTIER
WARDROBES IN THE 1920S.

Nobody knows for sure the origins of calling Stetsons "ten-gallon hats," though one popular theory states that the name came from the rough translation of the Spanish phrase "tan galán," which translates to "so gallant."

BANGTAIL

Wild horse; mustang

DUDE

Man from the city, inexperienced
rider, or wealthy Easterner
who goes to a ranch to experience
the cowboy life

★ ★ ★

"WHEN YOU BEGIN
A CATTLE DRIVE
YOU CAN'T EXPECT
TO SAY YOU ARE
FINISHED UNTIL
YOU HAVE VISITED
A FANCY WOMAN
AND PLAYED SOME
GAMES OF CHANCE."

— WILD BILL HICKOK

"THERE'S A LITTLE COWBOY IN ALL OF US, A LITTLE FRONTIER."

— LOUIS L'AMOUR

BAT MASTERSON

(1853-1921)

Masterson led as eclectic a life as any famed Wild West figure. He has been a famed buffalo hunter, participant in the Battle of Adobe Walls, lawman in various parts of Kansas, leading authority in Denver prizefighting, and columnist for the *New York Morning Telegraph*. As elected county sheriff of Dodge City, Masterson shot his brother's murderers, killing one and wounding the other.

At night, once the cattle were bedded down, a few men would slowly circle around and sing to calm any jittery nerves. Worried that a sound in the night might startle the cattle and cause a stampede, the men believed that the singing would soothe the cattle into a deeper sleep.

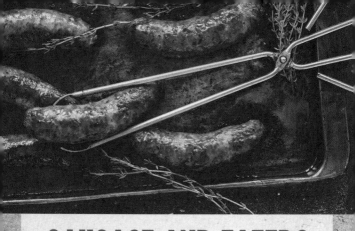

SAUSAGE AND TATERS

Serves 4

2 lbs. sweet potatoes
¼ c. water
1 tsp. salt

2 tbsp. butter
½ c. brown sugar
1 lb. sausage

1 Preheat oven to 375 degrees.

2 Peel the sweet potatoes and boil until soft, about 15 minutes. Once soft, cut into strips and place in a greased Dutch oven. Set the Dutch oven aside.

3 Mix the water, salt, butter and sugar in a saucepan. Bring the mixture to a boil and pour over the potatoes into the Dutch oven, baking the mixture for 40 minutes.

4 While the mixture is baking, cut the sausage into chunks. Remove the Dutch oven after 40 minutes and place the sausage on top of the potatoes. Bake the mixture for another 30 minutes.

According to the cowboy codes of the West, a cowboy is not to wave at another cowboy as they pass each other on horseback. A mere nod of the head in their direction will suffice.

UP TO A QUARTER OF ALL COWBOYS WERE FREED OR FORMER SLAVES.

BILL PICKETT

(1870-1932)

Originally a founding member of the Pickett Brothers Bronco Busters and Rough Riders Association, Bill Pickett reached the heights of stardom as a member of the 101 Ranch Wild West Show. He appeared in several early motion pictures, including *The Crimson Skull* and *The Bull-Dogger*, and popularized the cattle wrestling technique known as bulldogging. Pickett's death was a tragic one, as he was kicked in the head by a bronco and died several days later.

"There's nothing in life that's worth doin' if it can't be done from a horse."

— RED STEAGALL

"THERE ARE THREE KINDS OF MEN: THE ONE THAT LEARNS BY READING. THE FEW WHO LEARN BY OBSERVATION. THE REST OF THEM HAVE TO PEE ON THE ELECTRIC FENCE FOR THEMSELVES."

— WILL ROGERS

OWL HEADED

A horse that won't
stop looking around

MADE

A horse that has experience with a rider and is therefore thought of as being more reliable

JUDAS STEER

A steer that was able to lead the cattle to slaughter with ease

"A man on a horse is spiritually as well as physically bigger than a man on foot."

— JOHN STEINBECK

VINEGAR PIE

Serves 4

1 c. sugar
2 tbsp. flour
1 c. cold water
4 eggs, beaten

5 tbsp. vinegar
2½ tbsp. butter
Prepared pie crust

1 Preheat oven to 375 degrees.

2 Place the sugar and the flour into a saucepan and mix well. Stir the rest of the ingredients into the saucepan until mixed thoroughly.

3 Pour the mixture into the prepared pie crust and place in the oven. Cook for 30 minutes, lower the heat, and bake for another 30 minutes or until the crust of the pie has browned.

"AIM AT THE HIGH MARK
AND YOU WILL HIT IT.
NO, NOT THE FIRST
TIME, NOT THE SECOND
TIME AND MAYBE
NOT THE THIRD. BUT
KEEP ON AIMING AND
KEEP ON SHOOTING, FOR
ONLY PRACTICE WILL
MAKE YOU PERFECT.
FINALLY, YOU'LL HIT THE
BULL'S-EYE OF SUCCESS."

— ANNIE OAKLEY

HURRICANE DECK

The saddle of a bucking horse

POPPER

A flat strip of leather at the end of a
set of reins used to make a popping
sound on your saddle or chaps as a
way of communicating with the horse

Many cowboys believed that the use of barbed wire, also known as "The Devil's Rope," signaled the end of the Wild West.

BAXTER BLACK

(1945-PRESENT)

A rodeo bull rider and president of the Future Farmers of America (FFA) in high school, Black's affinity for western culture was on full display by the time he was 16 years old. He pursued a career in veterinary medicine, where he specialized in treating large animals for thirteen years. His celebrity took off from there, when he gained notoriety from public speaking and writing poetry. He presently hosts the radio program "Baxter Black on Monday," is a regular contributor to National Public Radio's "Morning Edition," and has over a dozen published works. He also writes a newspaper column published weekly titled "On the Edge of Common Sense."

Though not an immediately obvious feature, the creases at the top of a cowboy hat are largely unique and are meant to represent personal style.

★ ★ ★

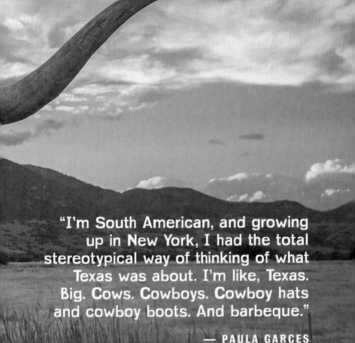

"I'm South American, and growing up in New York, I had the total stereotypical way of thinking of what Texas was about. I'm like, Texas. Big. Cows. Cowboys. Cowboy hats and cowboy boots. And barbeque."

— PAULA GARCES

WOOL WAS THE FABRIC OF CHOICE
FOR COWBOYS IN COLD WEATHER
BECAUSE OF ITS ABILITY
TO RETAIN HEAT WHEN WET.

JIMMYING
A BULL

Shooting an officer of the law

UNSHUCKED

Naked, a gun outside
of the holster

While the main function of the Stetson was protection from the sun's glare, it was also used as a cup out of which a cowboy and his horse could drink water.

BLACK JACK KETCHUM

(1863-1901)

A cowboy-turned-criminal, Tom Ketchum's life of crime began with a train robbery in New Mexico and ended with an amputated arm and death by hanging. Ketchum's gang, which had ties to Butch Cassidy's Wild Bunch, were implicated in several murders and even more robberies. He eventually joined the Hole-In-The-Wall gang, where he committed several more train robberies before being permanently incapacitated by a shotgun-wielding conductor who recognized him from an attempted robbery weeks earlier. Ketchum was captured the following morning and was hanged soon after.

"I never wanted my ability to take me somewhere that my character couldn't keep me."

— STRAN SMITH

CORN FRITTERS

Serves 5

3 c. oil
1¼ c. flour
1 tsp. baking powder
2 tsp. salt
½ c. sugar

¼ tsp. paprika
2 eggs
¼ c. milk
2 c. corn kernels

1 Heat oil in a heavy pot over high heat. Add the flour, baking powder, salt, sugar, and paprika into a bowl and mix well.

2 Beat the eggs and milk together in a separate bowl until the mixture is thick. Add to the flour mixture, along with the corn kernels, and mix thoroughly.

3 Drop the batter into the hot oil and cook until golden brown. Remove the fritters from the oil and drain them on a paper towel before serving.

On top of providing three hot meals a day, the camp cook was responsible for turning the tongue of the chuckwagon towards the North Star every night so that the drive would know which direction to go in the next morning.

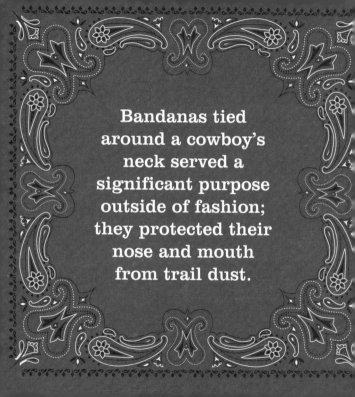

Bandanas tied around a cowboy's neck served a significant purpose outside of fashion; they protected their nose and mouth from trail dust.

MANTY

The waterproof
cover that goes
over a packsaddle

DUDE HORSE

A horse that is
slow and lazy

FLANNEL MOUTH

A smooth talker,
somebody who
uses fancy
language well

"I CAME IN WITH MY IDEA OF WHAT A COWBOY WOULD WEAR, BUT THEN I MET SOME REAL COWBOYS AND THEY SAID THAT I RODE THE HORSES WELL, SHOED THE HORSES, BUT NO GOOD COWBOY WOULD BE WEARING A PAIR OF LEVI'S. I HAD TO GET A GOOD OLD PAIR OF WRANGLERS."

— STEVE KANALY

"IT IS EASIER
TO GET AN ACTOR
TO BE A COWBOY
THAN TO GET
A COWBOY TO
BE AN ACTOR."

— JOHN FORD

HECK THOMAS

(1850–1912)

Thomas developed a disciplined mentality early in life, as he served as a courier for the South during the Civil War at the age of 12. He eventually became a Deputy U.S. Marshal and, along with two others, formed a group known as the Three Guardsmen, famed for bringing order to the Indian territory that is now known as the state of Oklahoma. They would apprehend more than three hundred criminals over the next decade, including members of the Wild Bunch Gang. Thomas was later named the police chief in the town of Lawton and starred in the one-reel film *Bank Robbers*, in which he and a posse chase down and capture the titular characters. Thomas died of Bright's disease in 1912.

THE FIRST
BIOGRAPHY OF
BILLY THE KID WAS
PUBLISHED JUST
THREE WEEKS AFTER
HIS DEATH.

"Talk low, talk slow, and don't say too much."

— JOHN WAYNE

GRAB THE APPLE

To utilize the saddle horn in order to avoid falling off the horse

★ ★ ★

THOUGH THE ELECTRICAL
TELEGRAPH WAS INVENTED
IN 1837 BY SAMUEL MORSE,
IT TOOK DECADES
TO INSTALL THE CABLE
INFRASTRUCTURE
NECESSARY FOR LONG-
DISTANCE COMMUNICATION.

★ ★ ★

MULESKINNER

A person who rides in
a wagon pulled by mules

LILY LIVER

Somebody who is cowardly,
scares easily

WESTERN BAKED BEANS

Serves 6

1 lb. dried navy or pinto beans

12 oz. smoked pork or ham steak, chopped

2 large onions, diced

3 c. chicken stock

¼ tsp. cayenne pepper

¼ c. dark molasses

¼ c. ketchup

3 tbsp. dark brown sugar

1 tsp. salt

1 tsp. pepper

1 Soak the beans in water overnight, draining the water when ready to use.

2 Preheat oven to 375 degrees.

3 Sauté the meat and onions in a Dutch oven over medium heat for 10 minutes. After 10 minutes, add the rest of the ingredients and bring to a boil. Cover the casserole and transfer to the oven. Bake for 4 hours or until the beans are tender.

4 Serve the casserole with a dash of brown sugar on top.

Other names for cowboys include buckaroos, cowpunchers, cowhands, and cowpoke.

KID CURRY

(1867–1904)

Known as the most dangerous member of the Wild Bunch gang, Harvey Logan is known to have killed at least nine lawmen in five different shootouts. Logan, who also spent time with Ketchum's gang, managed to escape the law by the skin of his teeth several times, often resorting to deadly measures to do so. He was eventually captured but escaped soon after and, following a successful train robbery with several others, stole horses to make their getaway. The owners of the horses formed a posse and pursued them, catching up and, following a shootout, wounded Curry. Wanting to avoid capture, Curry shot himself in the head.

The Pony Express, a system that allowed for communication between the east and west coasts, spanned almost 2000 miles between Missouri and California. Both riders and mounts were changed over at 12 mile intervals, reducing fatigue so that the mail could reach its destination in just 10 days.

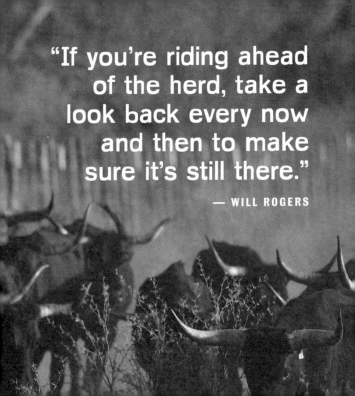

"If you're riding ahead of the herd, take a look back every now and then to make sure it's still there."

— WILL ROGERS

Riding another man's horse without his permission and putting on another man's hat are both considered violations of the unwritten cowboy code.

★ ★ ★

THIEVES AND NATIVE AMERICANS POSED SIGNIFICANT THREATS TO A SUCCESSFUL CATTLE DRIVE, THOUGH NEITHER COULD COMPARE TO THE WIDESPREAD DISASTER THAT THE BLOWFLY WAS CAPABLE OF CAUSING. INFESTATION ON OPEN CATTLE WOUNDS RESULTED IN THE SCREW WORM CATTLE DISEASE, RESPONSIBLE FOR KILLING MASSIVE AMOUNTS OF CATTLE IN THE WILD WEST.

★ ★ ★

CHUCKWAGON STEW

Serves 5

2 tbsp. oil

2 lbs. lean beef, cubed

2 c. hot water

1 large can tomatoes

1 clove of garlic, chopped

2 medium onions, sliced

1 thin slice lemon

1 tbsp. salt

¼ tsp. pepper

3 tbsp. sugar

5 medium-sized potatoes, quartered

Dash cloves

6 medium carrots, peeled and cut into 1 inch pieces

¼ tsp. basil leaves, crushed

1 can sweet peas

1 Coat skillet in 2 tablespoons of oil before adding the cubed beef over medium heat. Remove the skillet from the stovetop once the beef is browned.

2 Transfer the beef, as well as the water, tomatoes, garlic, onions, lemon, salt, pepper, and sugar to a large Dutch oven. Stir the mixture well and let sit for 2 hours with occasional stirring every twenty minutes.

3 Add the potatoes, cloves, carrots, and crushed basil leaves to the mixture. Stir, cover and cook until the recently added vegetables are tender.

4 Mix in the can of sweet peas and heat for another ten minutes. After ten minutes, leave the Dutch oven over very low heat until done serving.

SENIOR COWBOYS USUALLY RODE AT THE FRONT OF THE CATTLE DRIVE, WHILE JUNIOR COWBOYS HAD TO BRAVE THE TRAIL DUST AT THE BACK OF THE HERD.

"I ALWAYS WANTED
TO BE A COWBOY,
AND JEDI KNIGHTS
ARE BASICALLY
COWBOYS IN
SPACE, RIGHT?"

— LIAM NEESON

HONEY-FOGLE

To cheat or deceive

COME OUT AT
THE LITTLE END
OF THE HORN

To come away at a disadvantage

FRANK M. CANTON

(1849-1927)

A former bank robber and cattle rustler, the man
formerly known as Josiah Horner left his name
and his outlaw ways in Texas on his way to Nebraska
and Wyoming, where he took up law enforcement.
He served with the Regulators during the Johnson
County War in 1892 and, afterwards, moved to
Oklahoma to become a Deputy U.S. Marshal. Canton
twice got into long shootouts with outlaws holed
up in cabins and twice set them ablaze to draw them
out. He would eventually be granted a pardon for
his criminal past by the governor of Texas, to whom
he confessed his true identity, but chose to live
out the remainder of his life as Frank Canton anyway.

Cowboys were
so reliant on their
horses to carry
out daily tasks that
horse stealing
was considered
a crime punishable
by death.

Because of the abundance of cattle in the South and the urbanization in the Northeast, a steer worth four dollars in Texas could be worth as much as forty dollars in New York or Chicago.

"JUST 'CAUSE YOU'RE
FOLLOWING A
WELL—MARKED TRAIL
DON'T MEAN THAT
WHOEVER MADE
IT KNEW WHERE
THEY WERE GOIN'."

— TEXAS BIX BENDER

COWBOY COFFEE

Coffee Pot
Water
Ground Coffee

1 Fill coffee pot with cold water and ground coffee, adding one tablespoon of coffee for every two cups of water.

2 Bring the water to a rolling boil and immediately remove from heat. Add three to four tablespoons of cold water to the mixture and let it sit for 1 minute. Once the coffee grounds have settled, pour and serve.

★ ★ ★

A POKER HAND CONTAINING
TWO ACES AND TWO
EIGHTS IS REFERRED TO
AS A DEAD MAN'S HAND
DUE TO THE BELIEF THAT
WILD BILL HICKOK WAS
SHOT DEAD WHILE HOLDING
THOSE CARDS.

★ ★ ★

"Always saddle your own horse."

— CONNIE DOUGLAS REEVES

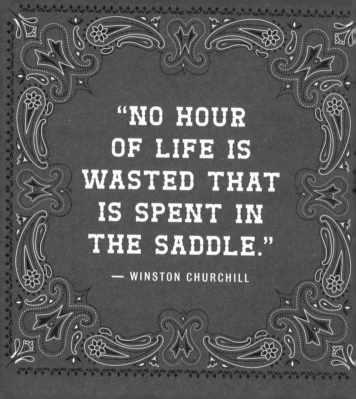

"NO HOUR
OF LIFE IS
WASTED THAT
IS SPENT IN
THE SADDLE."

— WINSTON CHURCHILL

"THE HORSE IS A MIRROR TO YOUR SOUL....AND SOMETIMES YOU MIGHT NOT LIKE WHAT YOU SEE IN THE MIRROR."

— BUCK BRANNAMAN

JAMES BUTLER "WILD BILL" HICKOK

(1837-1876)

Wild Bill's notoriety-turned-legend was the foundation on which his folk hero status was built, even if he was the benefactor of his own exaggerated tales. Legend has it that Bill defeated four men in a duel while sustaining only a shoulder injury, killed or captured a combined fifteen Indians in one encounter, and killed hundreds of men before he was thirty years old. Fittingly enough, Wild Bill was shot from behind and killed while playing poker in Dakota Territory. The cards that he was holding at the time of his death is now sometimes referred to as the dead man's hand.

A LICK AND A PROMISE

To give a job significantly
less than your full effort

INDIAN BROKE

A horse trained to be mounted from the right side (cowboys mount from the left)

"The first farmer was the first man. All historic nobility rests on the possession and use of the land."

— RALPH WALDO EMERSON

DUE TO THE AMOUNT
OF TIME CATTLE DRIVES
OFTEN TOOK, COWBOYS
OFTEN HAD TO
MAKE AN OUTFIT
LAST FOR UP TO
A MONTH STRAIGHT.

ON THE DODGE

Hiding out, laying low

MAKE A MASH

To impress somebody

"Real courage
is when you
know you're
licked before
you begin,
but you begin
anyway."

— HARPER LEE

COWBOY FRY BREAD

Serves 5

1 c. hot milk
1 package active dry yeast
2 tbsp. sugar
1 tsp. salt
2 eggs, beaten

4 c. all purpose flour, sifted
Vegetable oil
Plastic bag

1 Add the hot milk, yeast, and sugar into a bowl and mix well. Stir in salt, beaten eggs, and the flour and mix until doughy. Let the dough sit for 45 minutes.

2 Lightly flour working surface before placing the dough down and dividing it into tennis ball sized pieces. Flatten each piece and let sit for another 30 minutes.

3 Coat skillet with vegetable oil before adding each piece of dough over medium heat for 45 seconds on each side. Once cooked, store the bread in a plastic bag until served.

"I always say the English play Shakespeare, the French Moliere, the Russians Chekov, the Western is ours. It's our Shakespeare."

— ROBERT DUVALL

WYATT BERRY STAPP EARP

(1848–1929)

After Wyatt and his brothers served the law in various posts for a few years, they found themselves feuding with a group of outlaws known as the Cowboys. This feud boiled over in the Gunfight at the O.K. Corral, in which the Earps and John "Doc" Holliday shot and killed three of the outlaws. After the maiming of one brother and the murder of another in the following months, Earp formed a federal posse that tracked down and killed three more of the outlaws. That five-month stretch, as well as the widespread belief that he fixed a major boxing match that he himself was officiating, were more responsible for his fame than was anything else.

Because of their ability to exist in arid conditions, sixty-six camels were imported from the Middle East during the early 1800s as an experiment of sorts. The Civil War broke out soon after and, because of their perceived uselessness during battle, most were sold to the circus.

★ ★ ★

"A BOXING MATCH IS
LIKE A COWBOY MOVIE.
THERE'S GOT TO BE
GOOD GUYS AND THERE'S
GOT TO BE BAD GUYS.
AND THAT'S WHAT
THE PEOPLE PAY
FOR — TO SEE THE
BAD GUYS GET BEAT."

— SONNY LISTON

GREEN

A horse that has not yet been trained in how to handle a rider

ALMOST 35,000 PIECES OF MAIL TRAVELED OVER 650,000 MILES DURING THE NINETEEN MONTHS THAT THE PONY EXPRESS WAS IN SERVICE.

JOHN WAYNE

(1907–1979)

Though not an actual figure in the Wild West, the man who shaped the way we view the American cowboy could not be left out. Of his one hundred and forty-two movies, eighty-three of them were Westerns, starting with the movie *Stagecoach* in which he broke out as a leading man. The big screen was the medium and Wayne was the star through which the "Hollywoodization" of the Wild West took place, offering most of us a glimpse of a world we once knew nothing about. Quoted several times in this very book, Wayne epitomizes the American cowboy.

KEDGE

Feeling good, in good health
and high spirits

GRASSED

To be thrown from a horse

"My father's a protector. My father's old-school. He's a cowboy."

— PAUL WALKER

ABOUT THE AUTHOR

Jake Grogan is a Fordham University alum living with his younger brother in Astoria, NY. His affinity for cowboys was born out of watching Hollywood Western marathons as a little kid. In his free time, Jake can be found freelancing and listening to Lana Del Rey.

IF YOU ENJOYED THIS BOOK
OR IT HAS TOUCHED YOUR LIFE IN SOME WAY,
WE'D LOVE TO HEAR FROM YOU.

Please write a review at Hallmark.com,
e-mail us at booknotes@hallmark.com,
or send your comments to:

Hallmark Book Feedback
P.O. Box 419034
Mail Drop 100
Kansas City, MO 64141